"The Great Barrier Reef"

Ric J. Steininger

photographic artist

"An impression of the Great Barrier Reef"

Produced by:

Ric J. Steininger - Publications Pty Ltd

ABN: 34 335 605 933

Post: PO Box 12269, Cairns DC, Queensland 4870 Australia

Tel: 07 4052 1533 (int. +617 4052 1533)

Fax: 07 4033 5454 (int. +617 4033 5454)

Email: ric@steininger.com.au

Web: www.steininger.com.au

Ric J. Steininger - Gallery
Visit: Ric J. Steininger Photographic Art Gallery
63 Abbott Street (cnr Spence), Cairns City
website: www.steininger.com.au

Calypso Productions
Visit: Daypix Reef Imagery Centre
17 Spence Street, Cairns City
website: www.calypsoproductions.com.au

Panoramic photography, design and published by Ric J. Steininger
Underwater photography by Stuart Ireland & Lisa Conyers

Published June 2005, reprinted January 2006

© Copyright 2005 - Ric J. Steininger & Calypso Productions

ISBN 0-9581633-2-4   All rights reserved

Printed in China by Everbest Printing Co.

Text by Stuart, Lisa, Ric and Maggie

"Yet another day at work!"

An Introduction

It gives both Lisa and myself (Stuart) great pleasure to collaborate with Ric in presenting his third edition in the Impression series; "Impressions of the Great Barrier Reef".

On assignment together, on an island off Papua New Guinea, we soon realised our common passion to capture the magic of the tropical marine realm on film. This book is an expression of this friendship; Ric with his inspiring 'above water' photographs of the Great Barrier Reef and Lisa and I taking care of the breathtaking beauty and wonder of 'below water' vistas. Much to Ric's disappointment his panoramic camera doesn't like the water.

We hope that the images captured in this book help inspire a desire to experience the Great Barrier Reef for yourself and evoke a deeper respect and a stronger desire to help take care of our natural world.

Stuart Ireland & Lisa Conyers

The release of "Impressions of the Great Barrier Reef" has realised one of my long standing goals and desires; that of releasing a book that truly captures the grandeur of the Great Barrier Reef both above and below the water.

Lisa & Stuart

Lisa and Stuart's photographs are an inspiration to me, and they both share my passion and excitement for our natural world. It has been an honour to join together with two fellow photographers, both experts in their field, in order to produce this edition. Without their images, I could only tell a small percentage of the story.

In combining underwater photography with panoramic images from my Gallery Collection, I feel we have truly shown this natural wonder of the world in all of its glory.

Ric J. Steininger

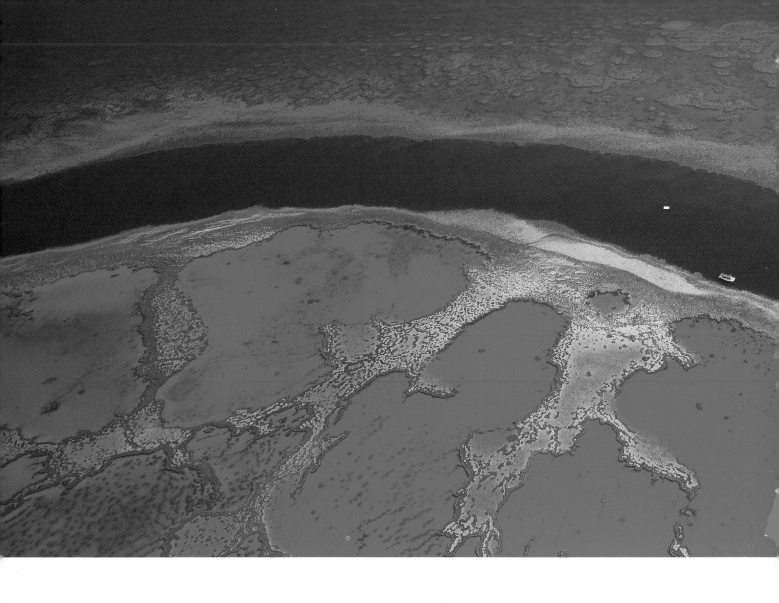

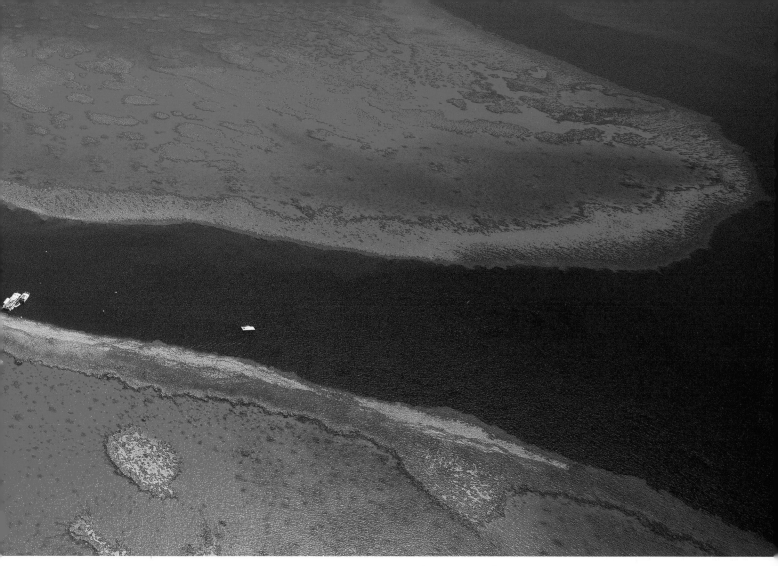

The Great Barrier Reef
A beautiful example of one of the thousands of individual reefs that together make up the Great Barrier Reef.

Green Island from the air

Above: Green Island, captured from a helicopter at 3000 feet, is a popular island for visitors from all over the world and is a short boat ride from the city of Cairns. Green Island is seen here in full grandeur with surrounding reef and aqua clear waters.

Next page: Nested on coral ridges you can encounter multitudes of Anemonefish, also konwn as Clownfish, each with their own symbiotic anemonies competing for space in this favourable habitat. There are several species of Anemonefish in the Great Barrier Reef.

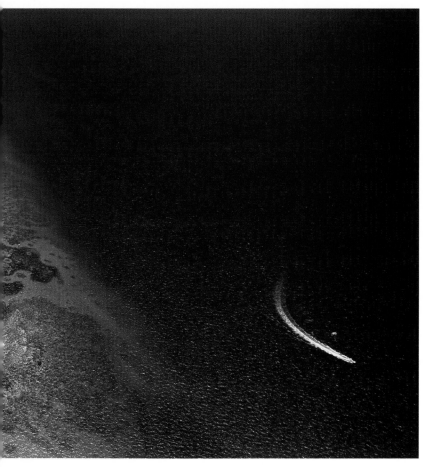

Top right: A typical vista of colourful soft corals dominate the seascape of many inner shelf reefs.

Lower left: Turtles are common throughout the Great Barrier Reef and can be seen in the shallow waters around Green Island.

Lower right: Six-banded Angelfish rests while waiting for a Cleaner wrasse to give him a clean.

Lower left: Quite harmless looking, these Stinging Hydroids can give an unsuspecting diver a rude awakening leaving a stinging sensation if touched. Perched on the reef top and sides where currents avail, they feed on plankton.

Hydroids are in the same family as the Portuguese Man-o-war but unlike their free swimming relatives, they remain attached in their mature stage. The colony is made up of a multitude of individuals, each with a specific role. Stinging polyps on the ends contain nematocysts which defend the colony while others have roles in cleaning, feeding and reproducing.

Lower right: Pecking at individual coral polyps, this pair of Butterflyfish are typical of the family; being fussy eaters they only target certain corals. An abundance of Butterflyfish is a good indication of a healthy reef. Butterflyfish have a clever camouflage - the 'false eye' in their tails confuses predators, who are uncertain in which direction the fish is swimming.

Right: Adding another dimension to the kaleidoscope of colours, these fluorescent orange Fairy Basslets dart about in the azure blue waters of an outer reef.

Michaelmas Cay

A sanctuary and breeding ground for a wide variety of sea birds. A popular destination to enjoy both the reef and bird life.

Left: Common to northern reefs, Giant clams can be found immediately off the shore of coral cays. Masters of self sufficiency, clams gain nutrients by farming symbiotic algae within their mantle. Attaining sizes beyond one metre, Giant clams are belived to live in excess of sixty years.

Sandy Cay
This is one of four amazing sand cays that can be visited from Cairns. Sandy Cay can even be accessed by plane.

Next page: A beautiful pink anemone houses this pretty Clownfish off a Port Douglas reef. Anemone and Clownfish have an interesting symbiotic relationship beginning from the egg stage. The eggs are laid under the anemone for protection from predatory fish. The anemone has stinging cells but also has a layer of mucus which is also on the eggs and when the eggs hatch, the fish coat themselves in the mucus. The anemone is tricked into thinking the fish is itself! Therefore the fish are not stung.

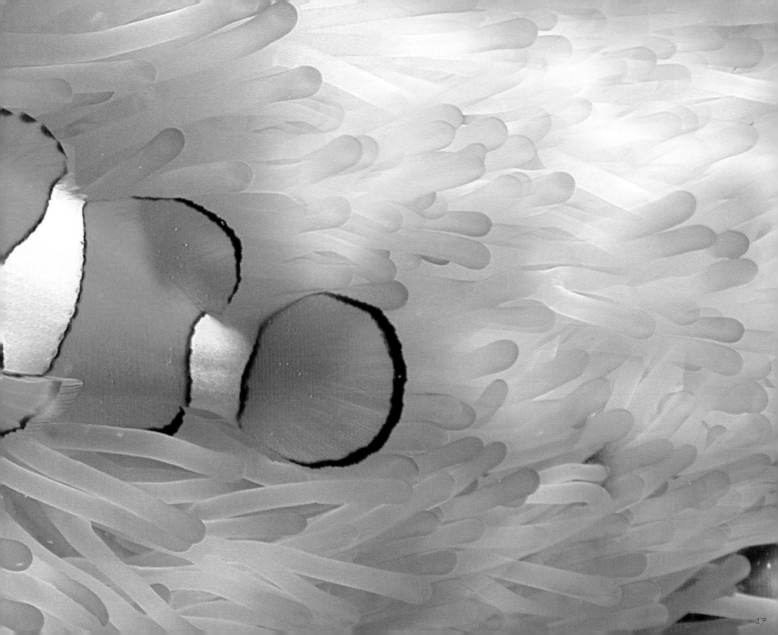

There are so many colours, sizes and species of Clownfish, always an intriguing and beautiful experience.

Above and previous page: *Spectacular colour when the anemone closes up revealing its textured and vibrant underside.*

Great Barrier Reef Anemonefish (Clownfish) nestled comfortably in it's home.

Low Isles from the air

Above: Low Isles, a tropical treasure found off the coast of Port Douglas. From the air you can see clearly the variations in the colour of the water as it leads off towards the deep blue ocean. A perfect location to experience a variety of sea life; like the Bannerfish and Batfish (shown on the right) that are abundant in this area.

Right: Low Isles photographed at water level with the coral reef showing through the water.

Scattered along the Great Barrier Reef are a number of ship wrecks, some dating back centuries. Coral and sea life quickly move in making them their homes (following page). The common and friendly Batfish make their homes in locations that resembles caves where they seek refuge. Also Lionfish (upper right) favour the same environment but for a different reason, they wait in ambush for prey.

Upper left: Looking closer in these sites you may find one of these tiny colourful Triplefins with their luminescent eyes.
Coral trout using a cave for a clean from a Cleaner wrasse.
Moray eel A menacing pose showing its razor sharp teeth, this Moray eel is simply opening its mouth to oxygenate its gills.
Barramundi cod unrelated to the estuarine Barramundi, this often shy and elusive fish hides under overhangs.
Large Queensland groper this gentle giant commands respect as it can attain sizes in excess of 2 m!

Cape Tribulation

Right: The splendid view of Cape Tribulation from the air, looking north along a coastline of pristine, untouched wilderness.

Below: Mackay Cay, one of two cays that are off the coast here. They make for wonderful destinations for diving and exploring.

(1) A school of Baitfish take refuge in a cave off Mackay Cay, and **(2)** a brightly coloured Flutemouth cruises the reef in search of food. Sometimes found vertical amongst the staghorn coral, or swimming behind similar coloured fish, the Flutemouth is a master of camouflage.

(3) & (4) Rays are commonly found feeding in sandy areas for small animals and crustaceans.

Far right: Cape Tribulation beach.

1.

2.

3.

4.

Left: The famous Cod Hole, a diving destination found north of Lizard Island. Known for the abundant numbers of extremely large Potato cod, divers have a chance to interact with the big fish. One of a few places where feeding is allowed, they have become accustomed to this regular routine.

Above: Lizard Island from the air, a natural reserve with an exclusive resort that caters for a limited number of guests.

Next page: Found hovering over a reef 'bommie', this large school of Sweetlips provide wonderful photographic opportunities as they watch you warily with their beady eyes. Like many reef fish, this schooling behaviour provides protection from predators.

Above left: Blue-green Chromis popping in and out of the coral changing colour electrically.
Above right: Never straying too far apart, this bright couple of Rabbitfish are most commonly found grazing on algae from the coral rubble. Rabbitfish pair for life and occasionally form large schools during feeding frenzies.
Left page: Darting in and out of their staghorn coral alleyways, these Blue-green Chromis move in rhythmic waves. They feed on zooplankton found in the current near the ocean surface.
Page after next: Large fields of coral provide the perfect hideaway for Clownfish and their anemone home.

"Tropical Islands"
Dunk Islands off Mission Beach, an idyllic tropical getaway.

Top images: Many species of Nudibrancs inhabit the reef. They gain their brilliant but toxic colours from their diet of sponges, hydroids and other specific foods.

Above lower left: Mating Nudibrancs provide a colourful jewel collection on the reef.

Above lower right: Flatworms in mid-water move like flowing Spanish skirts in dance.

Right: This Anemone fish seems queen of the reef as she stands guard over her territory.

Following page top left: Regal Angelfish change colour from juveniles to adults, starting off electric blue and changing to large coloured bands as they grow.

Following page right: The brilliant coloured mantle of this clam is from symbiotic algae. There are many colour variations of clams that exit in the reef.

Lower: A school of Fusiliers flee from pursuing Trevally.

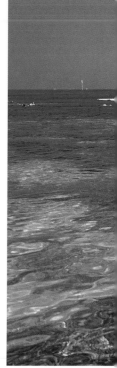

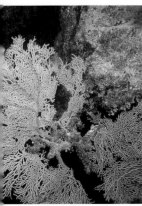

Top left: Arlington Reef, off the coast of Cairns. With a number of fantastic destinations nearby to visit, including sand cays and a number dive sites frequented by boats daily, the natural bird sanctuary of Michaelmas Cay, and many dive sites frequented by boats daily.

Lower left: A pontoon and two dive vessels anchored next to a reef.

Top right: A large pontoon that remains permanently out on the Great Barrier Reef with a vessel bringing visitors to the reef daily.

Lower images: Scenes of people enjoying the reef, snorkelling or diving.

Divers have so much to see and enjoy, slowly cruising around the reef. The Great Barrier Reef provides great opportunities for exploring and interacting with sea life in their own world.

Previous page: A very deep dive at Ribbon Reefs, mysterious blue.

Next page: Deep channels are lined with corals and fans, they provide great places for many species of fish to gather.

Page 56: Sealife provides vibrant colour to the reef: Damselfish find safety amongst the red fans and the sea floor with feather stars.

Top: Soft corals.
Above: This special turtle is very tame around divers which is a contrast to their otherwise timid natures.
Above lower right: Maori wrasse, known to locals as 'Wally'; an amazing fish with his independent rotating eyes. He has a love of interacting with humans, and acts like a loyal friendly puppy dog.

The various fans, starfish and sealife that display this brilliant red colour.

Whitehaven Beach from the air

Whitehaven Beach, simply spectacular. Coral is visible in the foreground, with the brilliant white silica sand beach behind.

Turtles of the Great Barrier Reef are just wonderful to see. Many of them have this beautiful pattern on their shell.

Whitetip Reef sharks often lie in rest in caves, their specialised gills allowing them to breath while not swimming.

A pair of Manta rays glide gracefully through the water.

We hope the images
in this book
give an insight
into the amazing
diversity of life
found along
the Great Barrier Reef
- both above
amd below the water.

The three of us
have enjoyed
sharing our passion
and excitement
for the natural world,
and in turn
we hope to have
inspired enthusiasm
and a greater awareness
of nature in all
who view this book.

... Enjoy!

Left: A snorkeller swimming gracefully up on the surface as a Batfish, which is only about 20cm long, swims in its own domain closer to the camera.

Rin J. Steininger (signature)

www.steininger.com.au

Photography is a medium of formidable
contradictions - it is ridiculously easy
and impossibly difficult.

Edward Steichen (1879 - 1973)

Books by Ric J. Steininger in his Impression series are:

IMPRESSIONS OF AUSTRALIA
Featuring images from around Australia.

IMPRESSIONS OF CAIRNS
Featuring images from Cairns and surrounding areas, from Mission Beach to Cape Tribulation.

IMPRESSIONS OF THE GREAT BARRIER REEF
Featuring images from the Great Barrier Reef including above and below water.